How To Use This Study Guide

This five-lesson study guide corresponds to *"The Actions and Personality of the Holy Spirit" With Rick Renner* (**Renner TV**). Each lesson in this study guide covers a topic that is addressed during the program series, with questions and references supplied to draw you deeper into your own private study of the Scriptures on this subject.

To derive the most benefit from this study guide, consider the following:

First, watch or listen to the program prior to working through the corresponding lesson in this guide. (Programs can also be viewed at **renner.org** by clicking on the Media/Archives links or on our Renner Ministries YouTube channel.)

Second, take the time to look up the scriptures included in each lesson. Prayerfully consider their application to your own life.

Third, use a journal or notebook to make note of your answers to each lesson's Study Questions and Practical Application challenges.

Fourth, invest specific time in prayer and in the Word of God to consult with the Holy Spirit. Write down the scriptures or insights He reveals to you.

Finally, take action! Whatever the Lord tells you to do according to His Word, do it.

For added insights on this subject, it is recommended that you obtain Rick Renner's book *My Victory-Filled Day — A Sparkling Gems From the Greek Guided Devotional Journal*. You may also select from Rick's other available resources by placing your order at **renner.org** or by calling 1-800-742-5593.

TOPIC

Why Do Some Deny Spiritual Gifts?

SCRIPTURES

Hosea 4:6 — My people are destroyed for lack of knowledge: because thou hast rejected knowledge, I will also reject thee, that thou shalt be no priest to me: seeing thou hast forgotten the law of thy God, I will also forget thy children.

GREEK WORDS

No Greek words were shown on the TV program.

SYNOPSIS

The five lessons in this study titled *The Actions and Personality of the Holy Spirit* will focus on the following topics:

- Why Do Some Deny Spiritual Gifts?
- Is the Holy Spirit Your Coach?
- How Does the Holy Spirit Guide Us?
- Do You Know the Spirit's Voice?
- Is Your Heart Divided?

The emphasis of this lesson:

From the time of his birth, Rick was raised in church and gave his life to Jesus at a very young age. Although the church he and his family attended provided a solid, biblical foundation and taught him a genuine love for lost people being saved, it didn't believe in or teach about the supernatural work of the Holy Spirit.

We can learn so much from hearing the real-life stories of others, which is why Rick devoted this entire first lesson to candidly sharing his personal journey regarding his relationship with the Holy Spirit. If you are a

A Note From Rick Renner

I am on a personal quest to see a "revival of the Bible" so people can establish their lives on a firm foundation that will stand strong and endure the test as end-time storm winds begin to intensify.

In order to experience a revival of the Bible in your personal life, it is important to take time each day to read, receive, and apply its truths to your life. James tells us that if we will continue in the perfect law of liberty — refusing to be forgetful hearers, but determined to be doers — we will be blessed in our ways. As you watch or listen to the programs in this series and work through this corresponding study guide, I trust you will search the Scriptures and allow the Holy Spirit to help you hear something new from God's Word that applies specifically to your life. I encourage you to be a doer of the Word He reveals to you. Whatever the cost, I assure you — it will be worth it.

> Thy words were found, and I did eat them;
> and thy word was unto me the joy and rejoicing of mine heart:
> for I am called by thy name, O Lord God of hosts.
> — Jeremiah 15:16

Your brother and friend in Jesus Christ,

Rick Renner

The Actions and Personality of the Holy Spirit

born-again believer but feel there is more to the Christian life than what you are experiencing, Rick's story will be a great blessing to you!

Rick was born into a Christian family, and when he was eight days old, he went to church for the first time. His father was good at documenting everything with his Brownie Camera, so there is actual, original footage of the first time Rick's parents loaded him up in the car with his older sister and took him to church.

Rick grew up in the church, going to Sunday School and worship services multiple times during the week. The leaders there understood what it meant to *be* the church. Rather than just being religious and only attending every week, church was a place where life happened for Rick's whole family, and he is so thankful for the godly fellowship he was raised in.

As a Southern Baptist, Rick was a member of the Sunbeams, which was a program for boys and girls from birth through the third grade that trained children to develop a firm foundation of the Christian beliefs found in the Bible. He was also in the children's choir.

Every night, Rick's mother lay at his side before bed and told him about Heaven and the life to come. Her words had a powerful impact on his life, just as your words have a powerful influence on the lives of your children and grandchildren. So never think that a child is too young to understand and take in spiritual matters.

Rick gave his life to Jesus at a young age.

When Rick first came under conviction of sin, he was very young — about the age of four. The reason it was so easy for him to understand the concept of sin was because his mother spoke to him every night about eternity. Her words made Rick wonder where he would go if he died. At the age of four, he really began to comprehend his need to give his life to Christ.

Shortly thereafter, Rick's church had a revival meeting. Today when people hear the word *revival*, they think of a major move of God. But back in those days, a revival was simply a series of meetings in the church that lasted about a week. A special guest speaker would come, and he would preach about things like hell, backsliding Christians, and the Second Coming of Christ.

On one of those nights, an evangelist preached about hell, and his words were so vivid, it seemed like Rick could feel the flames of hell just under his feet. Amazingly at five years of age, he really understood that if he died while in sin, he would go to hell, and the thought of that gripped his heart strongly. Rick said, "The reason I understood this was because my mother had prepared my heart by talking to me each night at bedtime."

That night after the sermon, Rick wanted to walk down the church aisle and give his heart to Jesus, but his mother was afraid he was too young and didn't fully understand things — but he did. Finally, the very next Sunday, after that week of revival meetings, the pastor gave the invitation for anyone who wanted to accept Jesus as his or her Lord and Savior. In that moment at the end of the service, Rick found himself slipping out of his pew and walking down to the front of the church to receive Christ.

As Rick took the hand of his pastor, whom he loved so much, the pastor said, "Ricky, why have you come forward?"

Rick looked at the pastor and then at his parents who were watching from the choir loft directly in front of him and said, "Brother Post, I've come to give my heart to Jesus." Then four-year-old Rick got on his knees and — with his Sunday school teacher on one side and his parents, who had come out of the choir, on the other side — he made his public profession of faith, giving his life to Christ.

Then, that very same night, little Rick was baptized in water. Because he was so little, the people in the auditorium couldn't see him in the baptistry. So his pastor put a chair underneath him that he could stand on so the people could see the top of his head and know he was really there! That was the beginning of Rick's life of service to Jesus.

Rick was taught to love God's Word and the lost.

In the church where Rick was raised, they were firm believers in the Bible, and their pastor had a fervent love for the Word of God. He would teach it verse by verse, chapter by chapter. He also had a fervent love for the lost and would talk to the church about their God-given responsibility to reach those who didn't know Jesus. For that reason, Rick's church regularly went into the neighborhood, knocking on doors to tell people about Jesus. They also had evangelism programs that reached people around the world.

Rick loved everything about his church and is so grateful to have grown up in such a community of believers. He believes that much of who he is today is a direct result of the church he grew up in. His overall view of the Church, what he believes about his responsibility to fulfill the Great Commission, and his intense love for God's Word are all rooted in what he learned as he grew up in that fellowship.

However, the church lacked knowledge and was closed to the supernatural work of the Spirit.

Unfortunately when it came to knowledge of the Holy Spirit, the church Rick grew up in was lacking. They understood that the Holy Spirit is the One who is responsible for birthing believers into God's Kingdom and that He produces His fruit in their lives. They also understood that it is His job to convict the world of sin and empower believers for Christian service — especially for sharing Christ with others.

However, when it came to the supernatural working of the Holy Spirit, particularly the gifts of the Spirit and His present-day movement in the Church, Rick's childhood church didn't believe in it. In fact, they were what is called *cessationists*, which is a doctrinal term used to describe people who believe that the gifts of the Spirit ceased or came to an end when the 12 apostles died. Rick's church believed there were no more supernatural manifestations of the Spirit taking place.

When Rick's church assembly came to passages like First Corinthians 12, 13, and 14 — which talk in depth about the supernatural work of the Holy Spirit in the Church — they just skipped over them because they believed those verses had no application for believers today. In fact, if anyone claimed to have a Pentecostal or charismatic experience, the church's congregation would laugh at that person and say, "Oh, he has bad doctrine. Whatever it is that he says he's experiencing is just a figment of his imagination because we know there's no such thing as supernatural gifts of the Spirit operating today."

Sadly, Rick's church dismissed the supernatural work of the Spirit and relegated His ministry primarily to the conviction of sin and the empowerment of believers for witnessing. Those two things were all the church allowed the Holy Spirit to do. Every week when the pastor came forward, after he had preached and had given an invitation for people to surrender their life to Christ, he would pray nearly the same prayer:

Father, I ask now that the Holy Spirit would fall on every unsaved man and woman as well as anyone that is living in sin — that the

Spirit would convict them until they come forward and surrender or recommit their life to Christ. In Jesus' name, amen.

Hearing the pastor pray like that gave Rick the mental impression that the Holy Spirit was like a divine blob that somehow moved across the congregation, and if a person was in sin, the Spirit fell on him or her, causing his or her heart to begin to race and palpitate. If he or she didn't surrender to the Spirit during the church service, He would chase the person to his or her house like the hound of Heaven, keeping that person up all night until he or she finally repented and gave his or her life to Christ. To Rick's young mind, that was the ministry of the Holy Spirit.

Of course, just before Rick's church members went out to knock on doors and visit people on Wednesday nights, they would pray and ask the Holy Spirit to give them power. But no one ever explained to Rick what the power of the Spirit was. Again his church really didn't believe in any powerful manifestations.

Rick became hungry and thirsty for more of God.

When Rick reached the age of 12, something began to change. Although he was still young, he had learned enough to begin asking questions. There is a marked advantage to raising your children in church. The best thing you can do for them is train them up in the things of the Lord early in their life. The earlier they start walking with the Lord in their life the better.

At this point in Rick's life, he began to think, *Surely there must be more to the Holy Spirit than what I have known up until now.* His hunger and thirst for more moved him to open his Bible to places like chapters 12, 13, and 14 of First Corinthians and to begin exploring all the territory in the New Testament allocated to the gifts of the Holy Spirit.

Meanwhile, Rick had an aunt who was a Pentecostal, which meant she believed in and fully embraced the supernatural gifts of the Spirit, and because she was of that persuasion, Rick's family kind of kept her at a distance. Doctrinally, they thought that she was just off, and whatever she was claiming to experience was simply a figment of her imagination.

Hearing the language of tongues piqued Rick's interest in the Spirit.

A day came when Rick went to visit his aunt, and when he walked into her house, she was listening to a teaching by Kenneth E. Hagin on an old reel-to-reel tape (this was before the time of cassette tapes). At that time, Rick didn't know who he was and had never heard of him in his life. But as Rick listened, Kenneth E. Hagin suddenly began to give a message in tongues.

That was the first time Rick had ever heard someone speak in tongues in his life, and it stunned him. There he was, standing paralyzed in his aunt's living room at age 14 as this man was speaking in tongues, and he thought to himself, *Oh my goodness! So this is tongues.*

It was around this moment that Rick's aunt came walking through the kitchen door and saw him standing in her living room in a state of shock. Her eyes grew large with concern because she knew she probably was going to get in trouble with his parents because of what he heard — but at that point it didn't matter. That experience put a hook in Rick's heart that made him want to know more!

Interestingly, when Rick heard Kenneth E. Hagin speaking in tongues, it didn't scare him. Today some ministry leaders and Christians are afraid that if people speak in tongues in church, it's going to scare unbelievers, but Rick disagrees. In fact, he believes hearing someone speaking in tongues will likely put a hook in people and draw them toward the supernatural move of the Spirit.

In Rick's experience, hearing someone pray powerfully in tongues *piqued* his interest. From that moment on, Rick began to see his aunt every day after school at about three o'clock. With his Bible in hand and a hungry heart, Rick would walk in, sit down, and say, "Let's talk about the Holy Spirit!" Step by step his aunt began to walk him through the Scriptures and teach him about the baptism in the Holy Spirit. And one by one, she gave biblical answers to all the doctrinal arguments against the gifts of the Holy Spirit that Rick had heard throughout his young life.

Finally a day came in January 1974, when Rick went to his aunt's house, got on his knees, and said, "Today is my day. I want to be baptized in the Holy Spirit."

His aunt laid her hands on Rick, and he was filled with the Holy Spirit. That day, for the very first time, Rick prayed in other tongues and began his search to really understand the Person of the Holy Spirit.

Rick's discovery of Kathryn Kuhlman changed his life.

Around the time Rick received the gift of other tongues, he found a radio program that aired every afternoon. It was of a very unusual woman named Kathryn Kuhlman, and every day when her program came on, she would say, "Hello there! Are you waiting for me?" And Rick says he would actually answer, "Yes! I'm here, and I'm waiting for you!"

Before Kathryn Kuhlman, Rick had never heard anyone talk about having a relationship with the Holy Spirit, and yet, she clearly had one. With great anticipation, he would listen to her daily as she described her interaction with the Spirit.

Shortly thereafter, Rick discovered that she was coming to his city to hold one of her big miracle services. Excited beyond words, Rick decided to join the choir her ministry was assembling, because the choir had the best seats in the building!

On the first night of the meeting, it was as if one could feel electricity being released when the service began, and it reverberated throughout that entire auditorium. Rick didn't know what it was at the time, but now he knows it was the anointing of the Holy Spirit he was feeling. When Kathryn Kuhlman came out on the stage, she said, "I'm just going to speak for a few minutes today," and as she spoke, Rick watched in awe as she fellowshipped with the Holy Spirit in front of them all. Rick had never seen anyone in relationship with the Spirit of God like that before, and it captivated him.

After an hour and a half passed, which had only felt like a few minutes, Katherine Kuhlman began pointing her finger toward different parts of the auditorium. One by one, she called out supernatural miracles and healings that were taking place. Soon after, the stage was filled with people who were testifying of how the power of God had touched them.

To wrap up the meeting, Kathryn gave an invitation of salvation to everyone under the sound of her voice. The response was nothing like Rick had ever seen. A flood of people came forward to give their heart to Christ, and of course, because Rick had been raised Baptist and believed in witnessing, this really impacted him. All these people were moved to give their life to Jesus, and all she had talked about was the Holy Spirit and miracles!

Rick was completely healed of a kidney disease!

Soon after that life-changing meeting, Rick heard that Oral Roberts was teaching a class at Oral Roberts University, and the class was called the "Holy Spirit in the Now." Rick jumped at the chance to enroll in his class, and every week he showed up, grabbed a seat on the front row, and hit the record button on his little tape recorder when Brother Roberts began the class. Every word he taught about the Holy Spirit, Rick captured on tape.

Not long after that, Rick found himself in a Kenneth E. Hagin meeting, and it was at this meeting that Rick received a miracle. But to fully grasp the weight of the miracle he received, here is the story in Rick's own words:

> When I was little, I had been diagnosed as having a birth defect in my kidneys, and it was so severe that I had multiple recurring infections. Doctors wanted to operate on my kidneys, but at that time in 1975, it was a very risky surgery that had perilous complications connected with it.
>
> Fearful that something tragic would happen, my parents decided to put me on medication instead of scheduling surgery. Later on, I attended a Kenneth Hagin meeting. In that service in the summer of 1975, Brother Hagin preached a message on the type of man God uses, and at the end of the meeting, he invited people forward who wanted to be divinely empowered for service. That's exactly what I wanted, so I went forward.
>
> As I stood in the front in the altar area, I waited to be prayed for with the others. In that brief moment, Brother Hagin prayed for me and reached his hand out toward me. To this day, I'm not even sure if he touched me or not, but the next thing I knew, I was on the ground. My legs just collapsed under me, and I couldn't get up. I felt waves of power like electricity pulsating back and forth, moving from my feet to my head and back to my feet and back to my head.
>
> When I finally stood up, I was completely healed in my kidneys! Although I had come forward for divine empowerment, which I did receive, I also received a miraculous, instantaneous healing in my kidneys. And I have never had an issue with my kidneys since then!

Without question, Rick believes in the supernatural gifts of the Holy Spirit. He is a recipient of the healing power of God, and over the years, he and his wife Denise and his family have seen many, many people receive miracles and healings.

All this began when he got hungry for more of God and began to pursue Him.

Soon after receiving his healing, Rick was led to begin studying John 14, 15, and 16 where Jesus elaborated about the ministry of the Holy Spirit in the lives of believers, and that is what we are going to focus on in Lesson 2.

STUDY QUESTIONS

> Study to shew thyself approved unto God, a workman that needeth not to be ashamed, rightly dividing the word of truth.
> — 2 Timothy 2:15

1. In this lesson, we learned Rick's story of growing up and accepting Christ as a child. What is *your* story? How and when did you hear the message of the Gospel and give your life to Jesus? What stands out most in your mind about the time the Lord saved you?

2. What church did you attend while growing up? What did they teach about the importance of Scripture, reaching the lost, and the Person of the Holy Spirit? What areas of their teaching do you appreciate for being biblically sound? What area(s) are you now aware they were lacking in that you needed to grow in spiritually?

PRACTICAL APPLICATION

> But be ye doers of the word, and not hearers only, deceiving your own selves.
> — James 1:22

1. The catalyst that propelled Rick to really search out and learn about the Holy Spirit was his hunger for more of God. Where are *you* in your personal walk with Jesus? Have you thought or said, "Surely there must be more to being a Christian than what I've known up until now"? How is this teaching stirring you to know more about the Holy Spirit and to grow closer to Him?

2. In Rick's life, the Lord used his aunt and ministers like Kathryn Kuhlman, Oral Roberts, and Kenneth E. Hagin to teach him about the Holy Spirit. Who has the Lord used — and who is He using presently — to teach you about the Holy Spirit? Who do you know

personally that has a relationship with the Holy Spirit? What is it about the way they live and the things they say that are distinctly different and life-giving?

TOPIC
Is the Holy Spirit Your Coach?

SCRIPTURES

1. **John 14:1-2** — Let not your heart be troubled: ye believe in God, believe also in me. In my Father's house are many mansions: if it were not so, I would have told you. I go to prepare a place for you.

2. **John 21:25** — And there are also many other things which Jesus did, the which, if they should be written every one, I suppose that even the world itself could not contain the books that should be written. Amen.

3. **John 14:16-17** — And I will pray the Father, and he shall give you another Comforter, that he may abide with you for ever; Even the Spirit of truth; whom the world cannot receive, because it seeth him not, neither knoweth him: but ye know him; for he dwelleth with you, and shall be in you.

4. **John 14:26** — But the Comforter, which is the Holy Ghost, whom the Father will send in my name, he shall teach you all things, and bring all things to your remembrance, whatsoever I have said unto you.

5. **John 15:26** — But when the Comforter is come, whom I will send unto you from the Father, even the Spirit of truth, which proceedeth from the Father, he shall testify of me.

6. **John 16:7-8** — Nevertheless I tell you the truth; It is expedient for you that I go away: for if I go not away, the Comforter will not come unto you; but if I depart, I will send him unto you. And when he is come, he will reprove the world of sin, and of righteousness, and of judgment.

7. **John 16:13-15** — Howbeit when he, the Spirit of truth, is come, he will guide you into all truth: for he shall not speak of himself; but whatsoever he shall hear, that shall he speak: and he will shew you

things to come. He shall glorify me: for he shall receive of mine, and shall shew it unto you. All things that the Father hath are mine: therefore said I, that he shall take of mine, and shall shew it unto you.

GREEK WORDS

1. "will pray" — ἐρωτάω (*erotao*): strongest form of ask there is; to urgently beseech; to passionately ask

2. "another" — ἄλλος (*allos*): one of the very same kind; refers to one that is identical

3. "Comforter" — παράκλητος (*parakletos*): a legal term for an advocate, lawyer, or someone who represents another; from the word παρακαλέω (*parakaleo*), a compound of παρά (*para*), meaning alongside or parallel, and καλέω (*kaleo*), which means to call; describes the Holy Spirit as One who is called alongside you like a partner; He is God's representative who falls in line with you, parallel to you, as close as one can be; pictures the Holy Spirit as One who is called alongside you to counsel, to advise, to teach, and to coach you

SYNOPSIS

In Lesson 1, Rick shared his personal testimony about his journey with the Holy Spirit. Although he had grown up in a denomination that didn't believe in the supernatural gifts of the Spirit, he came to a place where he knew there had to be more. The Lord led Rick to his Spirit-filled aunt, who answered his questions and was instrumental in helping him get baptized in the Holy Spirit.

After being filled with the Spirit, Rick discovered a daily radio program featuring Kathryn Kuhlman. Her teaching on the Holy Spirit as well as the meetings she held in Rick's city that he attended brought great transformation into his life. He later enrolled in a class on the Person of the Holy Spirit at Oral Roberts University, taught every Tuesday night by Oral himself.

Then in 1975, Rick attended a Kenneth E. Hagin meeting where he experienced the supernatural healing of his kidneys and was also divinely empowered for Christian service. With each new experience, his relationship with the Holy Spirit grew and his understanding of the Spirit continued to deepen. In this lesson, Rick explains how the Spirit is called alongside us to be our Counselor and Coach.

The emphasis of this lesson:

The Holy Spirit is the One God called alongside us to counsel, to advise, to teach, and to coach us. He is a Person exactly like Jesus in every way, and He is speaking to us all the time. To benefit from His coaching, we must listen to and put into practice what He says.

The Disciples Had Seen It All

One of the primary areas of Scripture describing the Holy Spirit and the different roles He plays in our lives is found in chapters 14, 15, and 16 of John's gospel. Here we find Jesus teaching His disciples about the Holy Spirit who was going to be sent in Jesus' place once He had died, risen again, and returned to the Father in Heaven.

After informing the disciples that He would only be with them a little while longer (*see* John 13:33), their hearts were saddened and troubled, which is why Jesus told them, "Let not your heart be troubled..." (John 14:1).

These men had been walking side by side with Jesus for more than three years. They were living the dream in relationship with the Son of God, the Messiah. They had watched Him heal the sick, multiply provisions, walk on water, cast out demons, and raise the dead. They had seen Him do so many things that John 21:25 says:

> **And there are also many other things which Jesus did, the which, if they should be written every one, I suppose that even the world itself could not contain the books that should be written. Amen.**

It is interesting to note that in the original Greek text, it says, "It is *not* possible, but let's imagine it was possible [that the world could contain books recording everything Jesus did]...." That's how many miracles, healings, signs, and wonders Jesus performed. The disciples had seen it all, and in addition to being forever impacted by His supernatural feats, they were also deeply impacted by Jesus' personal character.

Jesus Promised To Send 'Another' Just Like Him

To comfort and encourage His saddened friends, Jesus said in John 14:16:

And I will pray the Father, and he shall give you another Comforter, that he may abide with you for ever.

Notice the words "will pray." This is a translation of the Greek word *erotao*, which is *the strongest form of ask there is*. It means *to urgently beseech* or *to passionately ask*. The use of this intense form of the word "ask" lets us know that Jesus understood both the deep sorrow in His disciples' hearts and the seriousness of His request to the Father. It is the equivalent of Jesus saying:

And I will urgently beseech and passionately ask the Father because this is urgent….

What was Jesus' urgent request? That the Father send "…another Comforter, that he may abide with you for ever" (John 14:16). The word "another" here is very important. In Greek, there are two options that could have been used. One is the word *heteros*, which means *one of a different kind*. For example, the word *heteros* is used in the word *heterosexual*, which describes *a sex of a totally different kind*. *Heteros* is not the word Jesus used in John 14:16. Instead, the Greek word for "another" He used is *allos*, meaning *one of the very same kind* and refers to *one that is identical*.

When we insert the meaning of *allos* (another) into John 14:16, it is the equivalent of Jesus saying:

And I will urgently beseech and passionately ask the Father, and He shall give you another Comforter, One who is identical and exactly the same as Me. He will think like Me, talk like Me, and act like Me….

Jesus was telling His disciples — and us — that when the Holy Spirit comes, it's going to be like Jesus is still with us because He and the Holy Spirit are identical in every way. Sometimes people say, "Oh, how I wish I could have walked the earth 2,000 years ago to be with Jesus like the disciples." If you understand the word *allos* — translated here as "another" — you don't have to go back in time to know what it was like to be with Jesus because you have *one of the very same kind* here with you! The Holy Spirit is identical to Jesus in every way, and He lives inside of you!

The Holy Spirit Is Our 'Comforter'

Looking again at Jesus' words in John 14:16, He said, "And I will pray the Father, and he shall give you another Comforter, that he may abide with you for ever." The Greek word for "Comforter" here is extraordinary! It is the word *parakletos*, which is a legal term for *an advocate, a lawyer*, or *someone who represents another*. It is from the word *parakaleo*, a compound of the words *para* and *kaleo*.

First, the word *para* means *alongside* or *parallel*, and it describes *a parallel relationship*. This word could be used to describe a relationship between a husband and wife that are *para* to one another — living alongside or in parallel relationship together all the time.

The second part of *parakaleo* is the word *kaleo*, which means *to call*. When we join the words *para* and *kaleo* to form *parakaleo*, it is *one that is called alongside of another*. In John's gospel, it is used to describe the Holy Spirit as *One who is called alongside you like a partner*. He is God's representative who falls in line with you, parallel to you, as close as one can be.

Your relationship with the Holy Spirit is not meant to be long distance — it is meant to be intimately close!

The fact that the word *parakaleo* is the root word for the Holy Spirit means that He has a calling, and His God-given calling is to be alongside each of us in parallel relationship, as close as He can be to us. He is called to be alongside us in our good times and our bad times. He's there when we do what's right and when we do what we shouldn't do. He's with us everywhere we go and in everything we do.

When *parakaleo* becomes *parakletos*, it is *a legal term describing one that legally represents someone else*. This word can signify *an attorney* or *lawyer, a counselor* or *advisor, a teacher* or *coach*. Hence, the word *parakletos* pictures the Holy Spirit as One who is called alongside you to counsel, to advise, to teach, and to coach you. In fact, the word "coach" is a very good interpretation of *parakletos*.

The Holy Spirit Is the Greatest Coach of All Time

Think about what a coach does. He or she instructs and teaches you about what you need to do. Although they don't do it for you, they will tell you how to do it. For example, if you have a baseball coach, he won't hit the ball for you, but he will tell you how to hold the bat, how to position yourself in the batter's box, and how to watch for the best balls at which to swing.

Whether you're playing football, singing, or acting, your coach won't step in and do the work for you — but he will guide you to do it better. If you're playing football, your coach is not going to tackle your opponent or run down the field for you, but he'll coach you on how to function more effectively in your role. If you're a singer and you have a vocal coach, your coach won't sing for you, but he will teach you how to improve your technique, hit the right notes, and breathe correctly. Likewise, a drama coach won't act the part for you, but he will coach you on how to deliver the most riveting performance possible.

Take this concept into the context of what Jesus says in John 14:16: "And I will pray the Father, and he shall give you another Comforter, that he may abide with you for ever." In other words, Jesus said, "I will pray and urgently ask the Father and He will give you another coach that is identical to Me in every way. He will teach you, advise you, counsel you, and coach you in the very same way that I have done since I've been with you."

For three-plus years, Jesus had been coaching and coaching His disciples, and they were completely dependent on His instruction. In addition to showing them how to pray for the sick and cast demons out of people, He coached them on how to travel in ministry. He told them what to pack and what not to pack, how to behave when they entered a city, and how to leave a city that did not treat them well (*see* Matthew 10:5-16). You name it, Jesus coached them on it.

In Jesus' absence, the Holy Spirit assumed the role of Head Coach and took up permanent residency in the disciples, which includes us. "Everything I've done for you," Jesus assured them, "the Holy Spirit will do for you. He'll show you when to be silent and when to speak — even giving you the words to say. In every way, He will be just like Me, and it will be like you still have Me with you — only the Spirit will be invisible.

We Must Listen to the Spirit
To Benefit From His Coaching

Keep in mind, a coach is of no value unless you listen to him. A good coach can tell you what to do and how to do it. But if you don't put into practice what he says, his instructions are useless. For instance, a coach can tell you how to hit the ball, how to dramatically emote a part, and how to sustain a note while singing. But if you as the student are not tuned in and willing to listen to him and put into practice what he's teaching, it is to no avail.

Have you ever watched a coach just repeat the same instructions again and again, but the players aren't listening? Instead, they're talking with other players, thinking about what they're going to do after practice, or fervently trying to get the coach to listen to their "creative ideas." Players that aren't humbly listening never receive the benefits of the coach.

Likewise, the Holy Spirit is speaking to us all the time. He is speaking through the Scriptures, and if we open our spiritual ears, we'll also hear Him speaking to us personally in our hearts. He's coaching us on where to go and where not to go, what to give and what not to give, what to say and what not to say. Anything and everything about our life is important to Him, and He wants to coach us if we will only listen and obey His instruction.

Friend, the Holy Spirit is speaking. The question is, are you listening? Like Jesus, the Holy Spirit says, "Here I am! I stand at the door and knock. If anyone hears my voice and opens the door, I will come in and eat with that person, and they with me" (Revelation 3:20 *NIV*). The Holy Spirit wants to be welcome in your life, but He will not force the door open. If you will open the door of your life, welcome the Spirit in, and listen to and obey what He says, you will see the kinds of results that the disciples saw in the book of Acts. Their tremendous success was because they were fully dependent on the Holy Spirit and obeyed Him as their coach.

He's More Than a Feeling

It is vital to understand that the Holy Spirit is a Person — not a feeling. There are several Pentecostal and Charismatic people who are driven by their emotions, and that can be detrimental to one's relationship with the Holy Spirit. You may have heard people talk about having goosebumps or chicken skin when they felt the Spirit move in a particular meeting or Bible study, and those types of sensations can certainly happen at times when the Spirit is present.

However, tingling feelings going up and down one's spine and other emotional sensations are not what we are to look for, to long for, or to be motivated by. Yes, emotions can be good and helpful at times, but they are not to lead our lives.

Rick shared how he has strong emotions for his wife Denise and he really loves her. She's been alongside him for a long time, and she's going to be in parallel relationship with him all the way to the end. But whether Rick has feelings for Denise or not does not change the fact that she's with him and that she and Rick are in a very serious, long-term relationship together.

In the same way, you can't base your partnership with the Holy Spirit on your feelings, because feelings come and go. You are not developing a relationship with a feeling. You are developing a relationship with the Holy Spirit — the third Person of the Godhead. In coming lessons, you will see that the Holy Spirit has all the attributes of a person, doing things that a person would do.

Jesus Always Refers to the Holy Spirit as 'He' or 'Him'

As we noted at the beginning of this lesson, Jesus spoke a great deal about the Holy Spirit and the roles He fulfills in our lives in John 14, 15, and 16. And every mention of the Spirit is denoted by personal pronouns. Consider these passages:

In **John 14:16**, Jesus said, "And I will pray the Father, and he shall give you another Comforter, that *he* may abide with you for ever." Notice Jesus didn't say that the "anointing" may abide with you, or "it" may abide with you. He referred to the Holy Spirit as *He* — "…that *He* may abide with you forever."

Jesus goes on to say in **John 14:17**, "Even the Spirit of truth; whom the world cannot receive, because it seeth *him* not, neither knoweth *him*: but ye know *him*; for *he* dwelleth with you, and shall be in you." In this verse, Jesus uses the personal pronoun *Him* three times and *He* one time to describe the Holy Spirit.

Nine verses later, in **John 14:26**, Jesus declared, "But the Comforter, which is the Holy Ghost, whom the Father will send in my name, *he* shall teach you all things, and bring all things to your remembrance, whatsoever I have said unto you." Here again, the Holy Spirit is referred to as *He*.

Jesus uses the same personal pronoun "He" in **John 15:26**, informing us that "…when the Comforter is come, whom I will send unto you from the

Father, even the Spirit of truth, which proceedeth from the Father, *he* shall testify of me."

Moving on to **John 16:7 and 8,** Jesus talked again about the Holy Spirit, saying, "Nevertheless I tell you the truth; It is expedient for you that I go away: for if I go not away, the Comforter will not come unto you; but if I depart, I will send *him* unto you. And when *he* is come, *he* will reprove the world of sin, and of righteousness, and of judgment." In these two passages, the personal pronoun *Him* is used once, and *He* is used twice.

Then in **John 16:13-15,** Jesus described the work of the Holy Spirit once more, telling us, "Howbeit when *he,* the Spirit of truth, is come, *he* will guide you into all truth: for *he* shall not speak of *himself;* but whatsoever *he* shall hear, that shall *he* speak: and *he* will shew you things to come. *He* shall glorify me: for *he* shall receive of mine, and shall shew it unto you. All things that the Father hath are mine: therefore said I, that *he* shall take of mine, and shall shew it unto you."

When we carefully examine Jesus' references to the Holy Spirit in John 14, 15, and 16 in the *King James Version*, we see that He uses the word *He* or *Him* 18 times to describe the Holy Spirit. Jesus' exclusive use of personal pronouns to describe the Holy Spirit makes it clear that the Spirit is a Person. We can't have a relationship with a feeling, a force, or an "it." We can only have a relationship with a person — and that is who the Holy Spirit is! He is the Third Person of the Godhead that has been dispatched by the Father and divinely called alongside us to be our resident coach for everything in our life.

STUDY QUESTIONS

**Study to shew thyself approved unto God, a workman that
needeth not to be ashamed, rightly dividing the word of truth.
— 2 Timothy 2:15**

1. Did you know that everything about your life is important to God? Through His Holy Spirit, He wants to teach you, guide you, protect you, and provide you with His very best! Take a moment to consider what God says in these passages and identify some of the ways He involves Himself in your life:
    *   Psalm 18 (especially vv. 25-36)

- Psalm 37 (especially vv. 18,23-24)
- Psalm 40:1-5
- Isaiah 41:10-18; 43:1-3; 46:3-4

2. First Corinthians 1:30 says God has made Jesus our *Wisdom*. His Spirit is the voice of Wisdom calling out to anyone who will listen and obey Him. As you carefully read through Proverbs 8, what is the Holy Spirit showing you about the wisdom He speaks and the blessings that come from you listening to and obeying His voice?

PRACTICAL APPLICATION

But be ye doers of the word, and not hearers only,
deceiving your own selves.
—James 1:22

1. When you hear that Jesus urgently and passionately prayed to the Father to send us "another" Comforter — One who is *identical and just like Him in every way* — what does that say to you about the Holy Spirit?

2. As your "Comforter," the Holy Spirit has been called by God the Father to walk alongside you *to counsel, to advise, to teach, and to coach you*. He is to function like your *attorney* or *lawyer*, your *counselor* or *advisor*, and your *teacher* or *coach*. Were you aware of all these functions of the Holy Spirit? Which of these roles is the Spirit currently fulfilling in your life? Which roles do you need to invite Him to begin fulfilling?

3. When you look back on your life, who would you say was one of the best coaches you've had? What kinds of things did he or she say and do that impacted your life so powerfully? How did this person help you understand and appreciate the Holy Spirit's work in your life as your divine Coach?

TOPIC

How Does the Holy Spirit Guide Us?

SCRIPTURES

1. **John 14:16** — And I will pray the Father, and he shall give you another Comforter, that he may abide with you for ever.

2. **John 14:26** — But the Comforter, which is the Holy Ghost, whom the Father will send in my name, he shall teach you all things, and bring all things to your remembrance, whatsoever I have said unto you.

3. **John 15:26** — But when the Comforter is come, whom I will send unto you from the Father, even the Spirit of truth, which proceedeth from the Father, he shall testify of me.

4. **Acts 1:8** — But ye shall receive power, after that the Holy Ghost is come upon you: and ye shall be witnesses unto me both in Jerusalem, and in all Judaea, and in Samaria, and unto the uttermost part of the earth.

5. **John 16:7-8** — Nevertheless I tell you the truth; It is expedient for you that I go away: for if I go not away, the Comforter will not come unto you; but if I depart, I will send him unto you. And when he is come, he will reprove the world of sin, and of righteousness, and of judgment.

6. **John 16:13-14** — Howbeit when he, the Spirit of truth, is come, he will guide you into all truth: for he shall not speak of himself; but whatsoever he shall hear, that shall he speak: and he will shew you things to come. He shall glorify me: for he shall receive of mine, and shall shew it unto you.

GREEK WORDS

1. "another" — ἄλλος (*allos*): one of the very same kind; refers to one that is identical

2. "Comforter"— παράκλητος (*parakletos*): a legal term for an advocate, lawyer, or someone who represents another; from the word παρακαλέω (*parakaleo*), a compound of παρά (*para*), meaning alongside or parallel, and καλέω (*kaleo*), which means to call; describes the

Holy Spirit as One who is called alongside you like a partner; He is God's representative who falls in line with you, parallel to you, as close as one can be; pictures the Holy Spirit as One who is called alongside you to counsel, to advise, to teach, and to coach you; means to encourage, to beseech, or to admonish; also used in a military context to describe a commanding officer coming alongside his troops and stirring them up to stand tall and to face their battle bravely

3. "teach" — διδάσκω (*didasko*): means I teach; connected to the word διδάσκαλος (*didaskalos*), which describes a fabulous teacher and is the Greek equivalent for a rabbi; pictures a learning relationship between a teacher and a student, or a master and an apprentice, in which the pupil must be submitted to the teacher

4. "remembrance" — ὑπομιμνήσκω (*hupomimnesko*): a compound of the word ὑπό (*hupo*), meaning to be under or beneath something, and the word μιμνήσκω (*mimnesko*), which is the word for a statue, monument, or grave; to recollect or to brush off the dirt from the ground, pull that memory out of the grave, and put it on a pedestal so that you will never forget it; to bring to remembrance; describes the Holy Spirit's calling to remind us what Jesus has said

5. "testify" — μαρτυρέω (*martureo*): to give a firsthand testimony in a court of law; means when we surrender to the Holy Spirit, He will give us a firsthand account about Jesus, talking and talking about who He is

6. "reprove" — ἐλέγχω (*elegcho*): to prosecute in a court of law; describes a prosecutor in a court of law who brings forth evidence that is irrefutable and convicts the defendant

7. "speak" — λαλέω (*laleo*): to speak; to carry on a conversation

8. "glorify" — δοξάζω (*doxadzo*): to audaciously glorify

SYNOPSIS

The Holy Spirit fills many roles in our lives. From birthing us into the family of God on the day we get saved to presenting us blameless before the Father's presence in Heaven, He is the greatest gift in our life. Along with being our magnificent Comforter, the Holy Spirit will also teach us, reprove us, and bring to our remembrance everything we need to know. He longs to speak with us and clearly reveal who Jesus is, bringing Him great glory.

The emphasis of this lesson:

The Holy Spirit wants to be your personal Rabbi or Teacher. He wants to bring to your remembrance all truth, convince you that you're the righteousness of God in Christ, and testify of Jesus' goodness. But for you to get the full benefit of all He does, you must be submitted to His authority, listening to and obeying explicitly what He tells you to do.

The Holy Spirit Is Identical to Jesus

In our previous lesson, we examined John 14:16, where Jesus talked about the coming of the Holy Spirit and profoundly declared:

> **And I will pray the Father, and he shall give you another Comforter, that he may abide with you for ever.**

We looked at two important words in this passage, the first being the word "another," which is the Greek word *allos*. We saw that there are two possible words that could have been used for "another." The first is the word *heteros*, which is a part of the word *heterosexual*, meaning *another of a completely different kind*. Jesus didn't use the word *heteros* when He said, "And I will pray the Father, and he shall give you *another* Comforter..." (John 14:16).

If Jesus had used the word *heteros*, His message to the disciples and us would have been, "I will pray to the Father, and He'll give you another Comforter that is completely different from Me. He will be nothing like Me, and your experience with Him will be brand new and nothing you have been accustomed to." Can you imagine being one of Jesus' disciples and hearing that? That would've been very alarming.

Instead of using the word *heteros*, Jesus used the word *allos*, and the word *allos* means *one of the very same kind, identical in every way*. The use of *allos* in John 14:16 is the equivalent of Jesus saying, "And I will pray the Father, and he shall give you another Comforter — one that will be *identical to Me in every way*. It's going to be like I'm still with you, because He's going to think, talk, and act exactly like I have."

Friend, the Holy Spirit brings us the reality of Jesus. When we have the Spirit working in us and alongside us, it's like having Jesus with us.

The Holy Spirit Is Our 'Comforter'

The second important word we examined in Lesson 2 was the word "Comforter." Jesus said, "And I will pray the Father, and he shall give you another *Comforter…*" (John 14:16). In Greek, the word "Comforter" is *parakletos, a legal term for an advocate, lawyer, or someone who represents another.* It is from the word *parakaleo,* a compound of the words *para* and *kaleo.* The word *para* means *alongside* or *parallel* and describes *a parallel relationship.* What this tells us is that in addition to the Holy Spirit being with us and in us, He is also *alongside* us like a partner, walking with us everywhere we go. Just as a husband and wife are in a parallel relationship with each other, we are in a parallel relationship with the Holy Spirit.

This brings us to the second part of the word *parakaleo*: the word *kaleo,* which means *to call.* The use of this word tells us a few things. First, it lets us know that the Holy Spirit is called by God to walk alongside us, and because He is called, it means He is going to answer for how He fulfills that call. He knows His number one assignment is to be alongside us like a partner. He is God's representative who falls in line with you, parallel to you, as close as one can be.

When we compound the words *para* and *kaleo* to form *parakaleo,* it means *to come alongside us to encourage, to beseech, or to admonish.* What is interesting is that this word was also used in a military context to describe a commanding officer coming alongside his troops — especially just before they went into battle — to stir them up to stand tall and to face their battle bravely. He would describe the atrocities of warfare and tell them about the rewards of victory.

Again, this is all a part of the meaning of *parakaleo,* the root word for "Comforter," one of the primary names of the Holy Spirit. The use of this word tells us that when the Holy Spirit is actively working in our lives, He is speaking to us, calling out to us, and admonishing us. He's telling us to hold our head high, throw our shoulders back, and bravely march into battle. He is with us! Moreover, when this word *parakaleo* becomes the word *parakletos,* it means the Holy Spirit legally represents us. He is called alongside you to counsel, to advise, to teach, and to coach you.

The Holy Spirit Is
the Third Person of the Godhead

Another important fact that we learned in Lesson 2 is that Jesus used personal pronouns 18 times in John 14, 15, and 16 to describe the Holy Spirit. He never refers to the Holy Spirit as an "it," a feeling, or just an anointing. Instead, He uses the words *He*, *Him*, and *Himself* 18 times to explain the Person of the Holy Spirit.

What this means is that you are to relate to the Holy Spirit just like you would relate to a person. In the same way you relate to God the Father and Jesus the Son, you are to relate to the Holy Spirit. He is not a mysterious blob that just floats in and out of our lives. He has a personality with a mind, will, and emotions.

If you view the Holy Spirit as just an emotion, a feeling of goosebumps, or a free-floating force that exists in the atmosphere, you won't be able to relate to Him because you can't build a relationship with a feeling or a force. Feelings come and go and are constantly changing. The Holy Spirit is the Third Person of the Trinity that is fully God, which means *He never changes*.

Although feelings do sometimes accompany the presence of the Holy Spirit, that can't be what leads us and motivates us. For example, Rick shared how he loves his wife, Denise, and sometimes she gives him goosebumps and sends chills of excitement down his spine. But whether he experiences feelings or not, Rick and Denise are still walking alongside each other in an intimate marriage fellowship. Their relationship is not based on their feelings. It is rooted in a loving commitment to one another. Rather than relate to Denise as a feeling, he relates to her as the most important person in his life, and that is how we are to relate to the Holy Spirit.

The Holy Spirit Is Our 'Teacher'

Jesus tells us many things that the Holy Spirit is called to do in our lives, and one of the key roles He fulfills is seen clearly in John 14:26, where the Lord says:

But the Comforter, which is the Holy Ghost, whom the Father will send in my name, he shall teach you all things, and bring all things to your remembrance, whatsoever I have said unto you.

Here again, as in John 14:16, Jesus calls the Holy Spirit the "Comforter," which is the Greek word *parakletos*. This is *a legal term for an advocate, lawyer, or someone who represents another*, and because it is from the word *parakaleo*, it means that the Holy Spirit is *One who is called alongside or parallel to you like a partner*. He is God's representative who falls in line with you, parallel to you, as close as one can be to counsel, to advise, to teach, and to coach you.

The second responsibility of the Holy Spirit we see in John 14:26 is that "…He shall *teach* you all things…." The word "teach" here is the Greek word *didasko*, which means *I teach*. It is connected to the word *didaskalos*, which describes *a fabulous teacher* and is the Greek equivalent for *a rabbi*. It pictures a learning relationship between a teacher and a student, or a master and an apprentice, in which the pupil must be submitted to the teacher.

In the ancient world, particularly in Israel, if you were a part of a small group that was submitted to a rabbi, you were absolutely submitted to his authority. This was part of the requirement to be a part of the group. Under the rabbi's tutelage, one was required to totally obey whatever he said. And if you would really listen to the rabbi, then he could really teach you and take you places you could never get to by yourself.

Therefore, inferred in this word *didaskalos* — the root word for "teach" — is the fact that the Holy Spirit wants to be your personal rabbi — your *fabulous teacher*. But for you to get the full benefit of His teaching, you have to really be submitted to His authority. If you will listen and submit to the Holy Spirit and do explicitly what He tells you to do, then He will really teach you and take you places you could never get to by yourself.

The Holy Spirit Brings
All Things to Our Remembrance

In addition to being your Comforter and your Teacher, Jesus said the Holy Spirit is also responsible "…[to] bring all things to your remembrance, whatsoever I have said unto you" (John 14:26). This is a description of the supernatural reminding ministry of the Holy Spirit. It is how the writers of the four gospels were able to remember all the things Jesus said and did during His ministry.

The word "remembrance" in John 14:26 is the remarkable Greek word *hupomimnesko*, a compound of the words *hupo* and *mimnesko*. The word *hupo* means *to be under or beneath something*, and the word *mimnesko* is from the Greek word *mneia*, which is the word for *a statue, monument, or grave*. It describes something that should be remembered but possibly could also become buried.

When we compound the words *hupo* and *mneia* to form the word *hupomimnesko*, it means *to recollect or to brush off the dirt from the ground, pull that memory out of the grave, and put it on a pedestal so that you will never forget it*. It could also be translated *to put in remembrance*. Jesus' use of this word *hupomimnesko* to describe the work of the Holy Spirit means that one of the wonderful ministries of the Spirit is to remind us of what Jesus has said. He helps us dig deep and recollect or recall what we could not remember by ourselves.

Have you had moments when you needed to remember a truth from God's Word? Maybe there was a specific scripture on the tip of your tongue, but you couldn't recall it. In those times, turn to the Holy Spirit for help! It is His job to bring to your remembrance what you need to know and when you need to know it. Simply say, "Holy Spirit, please remind me of the verse or truth I need right now," and He will dig deep and bring to your mind whatever you need to know.

Although it is important and valuable to memorize passages of Scripture to the best of your ability, it is the Holy Spirit's job to bring things to your remembrance. If you ask Him, He'll pull it up, dust off the dirt, and put it on a pedestal in your mind so that you can see it once again and remember it. This is one of His ministries. Your job is to stay submitted to His authority as your Teacher or Rabbi, and He will really teach you.

The Holy Spirit 'Testifies' About Jesus

Looking once more at John 15:26, Jesus said, "But when the Comforter is come, whom I will send unto you from the Father, even the Spirit of truth, which proceedeth from the Father, he shall testify of me." Notice the word "testify." It is the Greek word *martureo*, which means *to give a firsthand testimony in a court of law*. Secondhand information is here-say and invalid in court. Only firsthand testimony has value.

The use of this word *martureo* — translated here as "testify" — tells us two things about the Holy Spirit. First, He will give *us* firsthand testimony about Jesus, telling us everything we would ever want to know about Him and more. When you are baptized in the Holy Spirit, you begin to experience a whole new level of understanding who Jesus is. The Holy Spirit loves to "testify" about Jesus, and He will keep talking and talking about Jesus.

The second thing the word *martureo* tells us about the Holy Spirit is that He empowers us to "testify" about Jesus to others. That is what Jesus Himself tells us in Acts 1:8:

> **But ye shall receive power, after that the Holy Ghost is come upon you: and ye shall be *witnesses* unto me both in Jerusalem, and in all Judaea, and in Samaria, and unto the uttermost part of the earth.**

In Greek, the word "witnesses" is the word *martureo* — the same word translated as "testify" in John 15:26. Jesus Himself said that the Holy Spirit's infilling in our lives gives us the power to testify and witness the Gospel to others. Now more that ever, we need to "…ever be filled and stimulated with the [Holy] Spirit" (Ephesians 5:18 *AMPC*).

The Holy Spirit 'Reproves' Us of Sin and Righteousness

What else is the Holy Spirit called by God to do in our lives? Again, we turn to John's gospel where Jesus said:

> **Nevertheless I tell you the truth; It is expedient for you that I go away: for if I go not away, the Comforter will not come unto you; but if I depart, I will send him unto you. And when he is come, he will *reprove* the world of sin, and of righteousness, and of judgment.**
>
> **— John 16:7-8**

The word we want to focus on in this passage is the word "reprove" in verse 8. It is the Greek word *elegcho*, and it means *to prosecute in a court of law*. It is the very word used to describe *a prosecutor in a court of law who brings forth evidence that is irrefutable and convicts the defendant.* Although the person charged with crime may deny the wrong he's done, by the time the prosecuting attorney finishes bringing forth the irrefutable evidence, that criminal is convicted. That is the word used here in John 16:8 to describe what the Holy Spirit does.

A sinner can't understand his sin by himself. It takes the supernatural ministry of the Holy Spirit to confront a person about their sin and reveal to them their spiritual condition. If you've been trying to witness to someone and it seems they just can't hear or understand what you're saying, you need to pray for the Holy Spirit to get involved and do His "reproving" work. His ability as a spiritual prosecutor is second to none, and He will confront that person with the irrefutable evidence they need to see to understand their deplorable condition of sin and need for a Savior.

What is interesting about this word "reprove" — the Greek word *elegcho* — is that it also describes what the Holy Spirit does for believers regarding righteousness. When we first get saved and are beginning to learn how to walk spiritually, we stumble and fall quite a bit. But even when we fall, God still looks at us and sees us as the righteousness of God in Jesus Christ (*see* 2 Corinthians 5:21).

Yes, we are all sinners saved by the grace of God, but God puts us inside of Christ, making us righteous in His eyes. This is very hard to comprehend with our natural minds, which is why we need the supernatural work of the Holy Spirit to bring forth irrefutable evidence that convinces us we are indeed just what God's Word says — the righteousness of God in Christ Jesus. Just as the Holy Spirit convicts and convinces a sinner of his sin, the Spirit also convicts and convinces a believer he has been made the righteousness of God in Christ. This is a revelation that can only be done by the supernatural power of the Holy Spirit.

The Spirit Is Always Speaking, So We Need To Be Listening

If you think that you have seen everything the Holy Spirit does for us, you need to think again. Jesus goes on to tell us in John 16:13 about another ministry of the Holy Spirit:

> **Howbeit when he, the Spirit of truth, is come, he will guide you into all truth: for he shall not speak of himself; but whatsoever he shall hear, that shall he speak: and he will shew you things to come.**

The word "speak" here is important. It is a form of the Greek word *laleo*, which means *to speak* or *to carry on a conversation.* Take time to carefully soak in what Jesus is saying here. The fact that this word *laleo* is being used means that *the Holy Spirit wants to speak to you and carry on a conversation.* The first and foremost way He speaks is through God's Word, but if you'll open your spiritual ears, the Holy Spirit will also communicate to you directly. He freely speaks to those who have an ear to hear what He is saying. But then in the next verse, Jesus tells us:

> **He shall glorify me: for he shall receive of mine, and shall shew it unto you.**
>
> **—John 16:14**

The word "glorify" here is the Greek word *doxadzo*, and it means *to audaciously glorify.* If you're one of those people who has a hard time expressing yourself verbally or physically when you worship God, the Holy Spirit will help you! He is a worshiper, and as you connect with and surrender yourself to Him, He will worship and glorify Jesus audaciously. That is another one of His ministries. He has come to glorify Jesus, and He will liberate you to praise and worship Jesus just like Him.

Next, Jesus tells us, "…He shall receive of mine, and shall shew it unto you" (John 16:14). This is yet another ministry of the Holy Spirit — the ministry of *revelation.* He wants to reveal and declare to us everything He knows about Jesus. He is a revelator.

Friend, these are all amazing features of what the Holy Spirit wants to do in our lives. That's why it's so important to truly understand who He is and remain submitted to and connected with Him daily — so He can fully work in and through us.

STUDY QUESTIONS

> **Study to shew thyself approved unto God, a workman that needeth not to be ashamed, rightly dividing the word of truth.**
> **— 2 Timothy 2:15**

1. The Holy Spirit is not a mysterious force that floats in and out of our lives. He is the Third Person of the Godhead who has a personality with a *mind, will,* and *emotions.* Look up these passages and identify the various aspects of the Holy Spirit's personality in each:

- Romans 8:27
- 1 Corinthians 12:1
- Ephesians 4:30; 1 Thessalonians 5:19

2. Jesus said the Holy Spirit will "teach you all things" (John 14:26). One of the most valuable things we need Him to teach us is what we are to say when witnessing to others. According to Matthew 10:19-20: Mark 13:11; and Luke 12:11-12, what did Jesus promise that the Holy Spirit will do for you when you're standing before others?

3. What instruction does Jesus repeat in Revelation 2:7,11,17,29 and 3:6,13,22? What does this say to you about the Holy Spirit that confirms Jesus' words in John 16:13? Pray and ask the Holy Spirit to develop a listening ear for His voice and a heart to obey Him.

PRACTICAL APPLICATION

But be ye doers of the word, and not hearers only,
deceiving your own selves.
— James 1:22

1. Do you have moments when you need to remember a scripture of truth God spoke to you? In those times, turn to the Holy Spirit for help! It's His job to "bring to your remembrance" what you need to know, when you need to know it. Simply say, "Holy Spirit, please remind me of the verse or truth I need right now, in Jesus' name." Then be still and listen. He will dig deep and bring to your mind whatever you need to know in that moment.

2. Jesus said we are to be His witnesses and share the Good News of salvation and redemption in Him. The Holy Spirit is the One who gives us this ability to testify to others. When was the last time you pushed passed fear and shared the hope of Jesus with someone? If you can't remember, pray and ask the Holy Spirit to give you His boldness to speak His words of love and truth to the lost around you, and watch with amazement what He does!

TOPIC

Do You Know the Spirit's Voice?

SCRIPTURES

1. **John 16:13** — Howbeit when he, the Spirit of truth, is come, he will guide you into all truth: for he shall not speak of himself; but whatsoever he shall hear, that shall he speak: and he will shew you things to come.

2. **Romans 8:14** — For as many as are led by the Spirit of God, they are the sons of God.

GREEK WORDS

1. "guide" — ὁδηγός (*hodegos*): a form of the word ὁδός (*hodos*), meaning a road or a path; a tour guide or one who knows all the roads; describes the Holy Spirit's ability to expertly guide us or lead us

2. "led" — ἄγω (*ago*): used agriculturally to refer to leading an animal by a rope draped around its neck, gently pulling or tugging that rope in different directions; also used in an athletic context to describe the agony between two men slugging it out on a mat

SYNOPSIS

In our previous lesson, we saw many amazing things that the Holy Spirit is sent to do in our lives, but for us to experience those benefits, we must be submitted to His authority. Being submitted means we are listening to His voice and are willing to explicitly obey anything He tells us to do.

Although obedience is not talked about much, it is very important. If you don't listen to the Holy Spirit, you'll forfeit His blessings and things will not go well for you. On the other hand, the Bible says, "If you are willing and obedient, you shall eat the good of the land" (Isaiah 1:19 *NKJV*). The fact is, the Holy Spirit is God and knows everything about everything. If you become His lifetime student, He will teach you all things and lead you into God's perfect will for your life.

The emphasis of this lesson:

Along with being our Comforter, the Holy Spirit is also the Spirit of Truth and our Guide. He knows all the roads of life — the best ones to take and the dangerous ones to avoid. If we'll listen to Him and allow Him to be our Guide, He'll lead us on the excursion of a lifetime.

The Holy Spirit Is 'the Spirit of Truth'

As we have seen in both Lessons 2 and 3, one of the names Jesus gives the Holy Spirit is the Comforter, which is the Greek word *parakletos*, describing the One who is called to walk alongside us and be our divine coach every day. It's interesting to note that Jesus calls the Holy Spirit our Comforter four times in John's gospel — John 14:16, 26; 15:26; and 16:7.

Another name Jesus assigned to the Holy Spirit is *the Spirit of Truth*, and He calls the Spirit by this name three times — once in John 14:17; in John 15:26; and in John 16:13. The reason for the repetition of these names is to really drive home the point that when we are interacting with the Holy Spirit, He is our *Comforter*, and He is *the Spirit of Truth*!

In John 16:13, Jesus talked candidly about the marvelous ministry of the Holy Spirit, telling us:

> Howbeit when he, *the Spirit of truth*, is come, he will guide you into all truth: for he shall not speak of himself; but whatsoever he shall hear, that shall he speak: and he will shew you things to come.

The fact that Jesus calls the Holy Spirit the Spirit of Truth means you can always trust Him. He will never mislead you nor misguide you. He is the Spirit of Truth, and if He has communicated something to you, there is a reason. If He prompts you to call or text someone, do it. If He moves you to give a gift, take on a project, or perform an act of service, carry it out. There is always purpose in what He directs you to do. But the only way you'll know the reason is if you obey His instructions.

The Holy Spirit Is Our 'Guide'

There is something else just as important in John 16:13 that the Holy Spirit does. Jesus said:

Howbeit when he, the Spirit of truth, is come, he will *guide* you into all truth....

Notice that word "guide." It is the Greek word *hodegos*, which is a form of the word *hodos*, the Greek word for *a road* or *a path*. What is fascinating is that when the word *hodos* becomes *hodegos*, it is no longer the word for a road or path. It is the term for *a tour guide* or *one who knows all the roads*.

It's the same word you would use to describe a person who would take you on an excursion. Thus this word *hodegos* — translated here as "guide" — describes the Holy Spirit's ability to expertly guide us and lead us. He knows the safest, fastest, and most pleasurable routes to take as well as the treacherous roads we need to avoid.

A Visit to the Kremlin Museum

To help illustrate the meaning of the word "guide" — the Greek word *hodegos* — Rick took us on a virtual, step-by-step tour of what one can see while visiting the Kremlin Museum:

> When people come to Moscow, they often want to visit the big museum inside the Kremlin. Although I don't do it much anymore, there was a time when I would take all our guests to see the wonderful Kremlin Museum, and I would be their tour guide. The reason they wanted me to show them around was, I knew all the routes inside that museum.
>
> For instance, when you first enter the Kremlin Museum, you walk through a vault door. What many don't realize is that the entire building is a vault because it houses so many treasures. Once inside, you walk up a set of stairs and turn to the left, and immediately you go into what is called the Diamond Fund. There you will see copious diamonds, emeralds, rubies, and the crown jewels of the Romanov family. The exhibit is simply breathtaking!
>
> When you're finished there, you walk up two more flights of steps, and you enter a circular room, which contains the coronation dresses of the queens of Russia. These dresses are spun of pure silver and are simply amazing. Because they are made of metal (silver), they're heavy and don't move. In fact, they've kept the same form from when they were put on display many decades ago.

Just across the hall on the other side of that circular room are all the garments that were worn by the priests of the Orthodox church during the time of the Czars, and these are also awesome to behold. One garment there has 250,000 freshwater pearls sewn into it. It is elaborately fashioned beyond words.

From that circular room, you make a right and step into another room filled with thrones. There is the Diamond Throne, the throne of Ivan Grosney, the throne of Mikhail Romanov, and the Double Throne of Peter the Great and his brother Ivan.

Turning to the right, you enter another circular room where you'll see the jewelry that was worn by the horses of the czars. Any woman would love to wear this horse jewelry! It includes broaches covered with diamonds and big, beautiful, golden-yellow sapphires. The broaches were worn in the mane of the horses' hair.

Leaving that room, you walk past the thrones and into another big circular room where you'll discover all the carriages of Peter the Great and Ivan Grosney, Ivan the Terrible, Boris Gudonov, and Catherine the Great. There are carriages after carriages to see and explore.

From the carriage room, you walk up a huge flight of stairs to the second floor where you'll see ambassadorial gifts that were brought by all the leaders of Europe to the various Russian Czars. The Bible tells us in Proverbs 18:16, 'A man's gift maketh room for him, and bringeth him before great men,' and that certainly was the case with the czars. No one came to see them without a gift. It was the gift of the visitor that opened the door for him to see the czar.

After visiting the massive room filled with all the ambassadorial gifts, you make your way back to the main staircase, passing the exhibition of Fabergé eggs, which are magnificent. Then once you get out of the Armory Museum, you will find yourself walking inside the territory of the Kremlin, and you will soon come upon the church where the Russian leaders were married. Right after that, you will see another church where they were buried and then a third church where they were coronated.

You may say, 'Rick, how in the world do you know this so well? How can you rattle off in such clear detail all the exhibits in the museum and the path to get to them?' The reason is, I've been there many times. I know all the routes inside the Kremlin Museum, and if you will trust me to be your 'guide', I'll take you along the right path and give you the most pleasurable experience you could possibly imagine.

Just like Rick can be a guide for the Kremlin Museum because he's been there so often, the Holy Spirit can guide you through spiritual matters and through life. You can lean on and trust Him to be the guide you need!

A Good Tour Guide Makes All the Difference

Of course, you don't have to have a guide to visit the Kremlin Museum. You can certainly go and explore it on your own, but that's kind of a hard way to visit because you'll have to figure out which roads to take and what hallways to go down. You'll also have to guess what's most interesting and worth seeing and what is boring that you can avoid. Most importantly, you'll need to find out where the bathrooms are, which can be quite a challenge because there are not many inside the Kremlin.

But if you allowed Rick to be your "guide," he would show you what you'd want to see and what you'd need to avoid. As your tour guide, he would tell you when to sit down and rest your back, and he would also let you know where the bathrooms are. As a guide, he knows everything in that territory.

Everyone enters the Kremlin at the same spot and with the same attitude of anticipation. Likewise, everyone leaves the Kremlin at the same spot, but not with the same experience. Those who had a good guide — one who knows all the right routes — had a pleasurable experience and left elated. But those who decided to do it on their own without a guide will likely have aching feet, a hurt back, and be in desperate need of a bathroom. Again, everyone exits at the same place, but not everyone exits with an enjoyable experience. A good tour guide makes all the difference.

In the same way, you can go through life calling all the shots and making every decision on your own. But your extremely limited understanding of what's in front of you will make it a tough and terrible trip if you are navigating the way on your own.

On the other hand, if you will submit to the guidance of the Holy Spirit who knows all the roads, your life will take on a whole new meaning! Remember, the Holy Spirit *is* God — He is all-knowing and all-powerful. He's already been where you're going, and He knows what God has planned for your life down to the smallest detail. Likewise, He knows what the devil has planned for you. If you'll allow the Holy Spirit to be your "guide," He will circumvent the enemy's attacks, and when you leave this planet to go to Heaven, you will be able to say, "Wow! What a ride!"

The best decision you can make is to daily submit to the Holy Spirit and let Him be your "guide."

What Does It Mean
To Be 'Led' by the Spirit?

If you are saved, you have the ability to be led by the Holy Spirit. In fact, one proof of salvation is that the Holy Spirit leads you. The apostle Paul makes this clear in Romans 8:14 where he tells us plainly:

> **For as many as are led by the Spirit of God, they are the sons of God.**

The word "led" in this verse is very important. It is the Greek word *ago*, and in the ancient world it was used in two basic ways: agriculturally and athletically. In the agricultural sense, the word *ago* was used to refer to *leading an animal by a rope draped around its neck, gently pulling or tugging that rope in different directions.*

Rather than drag an animal around, you would teach and train the animal — such as a cow, a donkey, a mule, or a camel — to follow you by gently tugging on a rope that was wrapped around its neck. This is a picture of the meaning of the word *ago* — translated in Romans 8:14 as "led."

Here is a real-life story from Rick illustrating the meaning of the word "led":

> When Denise and I first moved to the territory of the former Soviet Union, we lived in a very small town, and just outside the town were sprawling farmlands.

> There was a little lady in our neighborhood who would walk her cow every day, and I had never seen anything quite like that. Each

morning, she would put a rope around the neck of her cow and then barely tug on it, and the cow would follow her.

Again and again, I watched as she led the cow to a particular place, pulled a stake out of her pocket, nailed it into the ground, wrapped the end of the rope around the stake, and just left the cow there. The cow wouldn't move. It just stayed where it was led until the evening when the little woman came back, pulled up the steak, grabbed hold of the rope, and led the cow back home. Amazingly, that huge animal would obediently follow that tiny woman every time.

As I watched this lady walk her cow every day during those years, I remember thinking about Romans 8:14, which says, 'For as many as are led by the Spirit of God, they are the sons of God.' The word 'led' in this verse is the Greek word *ago*, and it means *to lead with a rope wrapped around the neck*.

One day, curiosity got the best of me, and I said to her, 'What is wrong with that cow? It just obediently follows you wherever you take it. It's so big, and you're so little by comparison. That cow is so strong it could easily pull up that stake and be on its way, but it just stays where you led it.'

My neighbor smiled and said, 'Rick, these cows have been trained to follow from the time they were very young. They understand that they are to stay where they are led.'

What a vivid revelation! In the same way, we must be trained to follow the leading of the Holy Spirit when we first get saved. We need to learn what His gentle tug feels like and learn to trust that when He leads us somewhere, we need to stay put and not move until He returns to lead us somewhere else.

Like these well-trained animals, the Holy Spirit wants to lead us by a gentle tug in the direction He knows is best for us. Unfortunately, many Christians want to be led by something dramatic, like an angelic appearance, a prophetic dream or vision, or a flash of lightning and a thunderclap. Although it is certainly exciting when we receive such vivid direction, the kind of leading we're going to receive most often will be a gentle tug on our heart by the Holy Spirit. It's our job to learn to recognize and be sensitive to His tug on our heart.

Being Led by the Spirit
Is Sometimes a Wrestling Match

In addition to the agricultural use of the word, the Greek word *ago* was also used in an athletic context to describe *the agony between two men slugging it out on a mat*. As they wrestled, trying to get the upper hand and pin their opponent, both men would hurl each other to the ground, attempting to master one another.

The fact that this word *ago* — translated in Romans 8:14 as "led" — also carries the idea of an athletic struggle, importantly tells us that when the Holy Spirit is trying to lead us, there is often a contest or wrestling match between our heart and our head.

As the Holy Spirit gently tugs on your heart, trying to lead you to do the right thing, go to the right place, or simply stay put, your head argues against Him, saying things like, *I don't like what I'm being told, and I don't want to do it!*

Hence, a wrestling match ensues where our carnal, unrenewed mind argues with our heart. Ultimately, we have to learn to obey the Holy Spirit and trust His leading. If we will follow His gentle prompting, where He leads us will be a great blessing.

A Valuable Lesson in Listening to the Spirit's Voice

To help you understand the vital importance of obeying the still, small voice of the Spirit, Rick candidly shared this sobering situation that took place many years ago while he was traveling. It reveals how being "led" by the Holy Spirit can sometimes be a real wrestling match.

> Many years ago, Denise and I were ministering in Chicago, and on one afternoon, we lay down to get some rest before we went to the evening service. As I lay on the bed, I began to be deeply disturbed in my heart and sensed I wasn't supposed to leave the room that night. But my mind said, *Why would the Holy Spirit want me to stay in this room when I could go to the meeting and receive wonderful ministry?*
>
> As we got up and got dressed, I said to Denise, 'I don't know why, but I feel the Holy Spirit tugging on my heart, urging me not to

leave this room tonight. It makes no logical sense that He would tell me to do that.' But Denise didn't have the same leading.

Thus a war began between my heart and my head. After a while, I finally convinced myself that the thoughts to stay in the room were sheer nonsense. *This must be my imagination*, I thought. So I overrode the uneasiness in my spirit and made the decision to go to the meeting.

As Denise and I rode across town to the church, the whole way there I was grieved and weighed down on the inside. Several times I turned to Denise and said, 'I don't know why, but I feel like this car needs to turn around and take me back to the hotel room. For some reason, I'm supposed to be in that room tonight.' Then my mind would kick in and reason it away, saying, *No, that doesn't make any sense. Why would God want me to sit in a room by myself when I could be in a great meeting receiving wonderful ministry?*

Finally, we made it to the church where we greeted our friends with handshakes and hugs, but just as we all turned to walk into the auditorium for the meeting, the intensity of the inward grief became even stronger. In that moment, I said, 'Denise, I don't know what's going on, but for some reason I feel I'm supposed to be in our hotel room tonight. I feel like the Holy Spirit is telling me to go back to the room and get there as fast as I can. I can't go into the service.'

I quickly reconnected with our driver and asked him to please take me back to my hotel. As we made our way back across town, I realized I was going to miss dinner, so I asked the driver to pull into a fast-food restaurant so I could get something to eat. I then took my time and walked over to a nearby convenience store and bought some toothpaste and then slowly made my way back to the car.

When I got back to the hotel and walked into the lobby, the receptionist said, 'Why are you back from the meeting so early?' Rather than try to explain to her about feeling led that I was supposed to be in my room, I chose to visit with her for a little while and then make my way to the elevator and back up to our room.

At that point, a great deal of time had passed. When I finally made it to our floor and walked down the hallway, I noticed that the door to our room was slightly ajar. I walked into the room, and it looked as though a whirlwind had come through. Our suitcases were open, and our clothes were thrown around everywhere. Immediately, I noticed Denise's jewelry box had been tossed to the floor, and it was empty. Nothing was left but some cheap custom jewelry scattered around.

Frantic, I turned and looked over at the desk where I had left my computer and my work bag. Both were now gone. Of all our possessions, these were extremely important. My work bag contained my passport and all our legal documents, and on my computer were five unpublished books that I was writing — and I had no additional copies.

As I stood there in a state of shock and gazed around the room, it took me a few seconds to realize we had been robbed. Someone came in after we had left and ransacked the room. This person had gone through all our luggage and stolen my computer, my workbag, and all of Denise's beautiful jewelry — some of which was brand new. Everything of value was taken, and we felt so violated.

Instantly, I heard the still voice of the Holy Spirit say, *Now you know why I was leading you to stay in the room.* I realized if I had stayed in the room as I had been led, the thief would have never entered. He would have knocked on the door, but when he found someone was there, he wouldn't have come in. If I had stayed in the room like I felt led to do, that event would have never taken place. I learned a valuable lesson from that experience: Always listen to and obey the guiding voice of the Holy Spirit, and catastrophes like this can be avoided.

Remember, the Holy Spirit is your Guide — your *hodegos*. He knows all the roads and is keenly aware of what's going to happen *before* it takes place. He knows what God has planned as well as what the enemy has planned. Therefore, He knows what actions you need to take and which ones you need to avoid. He will tell you when to go and when to stop, what to say and what not to say.

If you will obey the Holy Spirit and let Him be your Guide, He will direct you down the right roads and help you escape the traps the enemy has planned. The Spirit will gently tug on your heart and lead you to make the healthiest choices you can make in every area of your life. He is the Spirit of Truth that you can fully trust, and He will guide you in such a way that your life's journey will be a pleasurable experience!

STUDY QUESTIONS

Study to shew thyself approved unto God, a workman that needeth not to be ashamed, rightly dividing the word of truth.
— 2 Timothy 2:15

1. Although it's exciting to receive a vivid prophetic word, dream, or vision from the Holy Spirit, He often leads us by *a still small voice* (*see* in 1 Kings 19:9-13) or *a gentle tug on our heart*. Many times, that gentle tug comes in the form of God's *peace*. Carefully meditate on **Colossians 3:15** in the *Amplified Classic* and jot down what the Holy Spirit shows you about being led by His peace. What does the *presence* of God's peace in a situation mean? How about the *absence* of peace?

    And let the peace (soul harmony which comes) from Christ rule (act as umpire continually) in your hearts [deciding and settling with finality all questions that arise in your minds, in that peaceful state] to which as [members of Christ's] one body you were also called [to live]. And be thankful (appreciative), [giving praise to God always].

2. Attempting to figure out everything in your life is exhausting and overwhelming. Thankfully, you don't have to! God knows the beginning from the end (*see* Isaiah 46:9-10) and will take care of everything as you learn to trust in Him. Take time to read Proverbs 3:5-8 in a few different translations and write out the version that God really brings to life.

3. As you move forward and make plans for your life, consider what God says in Proverbs 16:1-3,9; 19:21; 20:24; 127:1; and James 4:13-16. How do these passages bring balance and help shape your decision-making?

PRACTICAL APPLICATION

But be ye doers of the word, and not hearers only,
deceiving your own selves.
—James 1:22

1. Often, the Holy Spirit's guidance comes in the form of *a gentle tug on our heart.* Can you recall a time when you felt the Spirit gently leading you to do or *not* do something? What was it, and did you follow His leading? If not, why? If you obeyed, what happened as a result and what did you learn from the situation?

2. If the Holy Spirit has told you to do something, there's a reason. Has He prompted you to call or text someone? Has He moved you to give a gift, take on a project, or perform an act of service? What has He been impressing on you to do that hasn't gone away? Have you done it? Realize there is always purpose in what He directs you to do. But the only way you'll know the reason is if you obey His instructions.

LESSON 5

TOPIC

Is Your Heart Divided?

SCRIPTURES

1. **James 4:4** — Ye adulterers and adulteresses, know ye not that the friendship of the world is enmity with God? whosoever therefore will be a friend of the world is the enemy of God.

2. **James 4:5** — Do ye think that the scripture saith in vain, The spirit that dwelleth in us lusteth to envy?

GREEK WORDS

1. "friendship" — φιλία (*philia*): friendship; describes a reciprocal relationship or affection

2. "world" — κόσμος (*kosmos*): every system or institution of the world, such as fashion, entertainment, education, politics, and more; every part of the world

3. "enmity" — ἔχθρα (*ecthra*): hostility or opposition between two people; used in the Bible to describe the hostile relationship between Herod the Great and Pilate

4. "will be" — βούλομαι (*boulomai*): means I advise or I counsel; pictures the process of coaxing oneself or counseling oneself into something; describes a believer who was once white hot with love for Jesus but over time has gradually talked himself out of relationship with Jesus and back into relationship with the world

5. "dwell" — κατοικέω (*katoikeo*): a compound of κατ (*kat*) and οἰκέω (*oikeo*); κατ (*kat*) is from the word κατά (*kata*), meaning down, and οἰκέω (*oikeo*) is from the Greek word οἶκος (*oikos*), meaning house, but in the form οἰκέω (*oikeo*), it means to live; together, κατοικέω (*katoikeo*) describes a person settled down in a new home making it his permanent residency

6. "lust" — ἐπιποθέω (*epipotheo*): depicts someone longing for something with such intensity that he is doubled over, hankering for it, longing for it, and pining for it

7. "envy" — φθόνος (*phthonos*): intense jealousy, such as what a person feels when he discovers his wife has committed adultery; pictures a rescue operation or plan in which the husband is willing to do whatever it takes to break the affair and bring his wife back home

SYNOPSIS

As we established in previous lessons, the Holy Spirit is not an "it," a force, or a feeling. He is the mighty Third Person of the Trinity who is fully God and has a distinct personality. Romans 8:27 reveals that the Spirit of God has a *mind*; First Corinthians 12:11 says He has a *will*; and Ephesians 4:30 and First Thessalonians 5:19 tell us the Spirit has *emotions*.

In this lesson, we'll take a closer look at the consequences of giving our devotion to someone or something other than God. We'll also discover that the Holy Spirit is not a neutral party, and once He moves into our heart, He is not planning to leave.

The emphasis of this lesson:

When we give our affection and devotion more to the world and its possessions than to Jesus, God calls it spiritual adultery. This behavior, which comes on gradually through unhealthy self-talk, makes us hostile

enemies of God. The Holy Spirit, who has taken up permanent residency in us, yearns jealously to be number one and will fight to stay first in our lives.

James Called His Readers *Adulteresses*

When we come to James 4, there are two verses that speak about the Holy Spirit having feelings that we need to understand. The James who wrote this letter is the half-brother of Jesus, and he was writing to a group of believers that had become very discouraged. Their actions were grieving the Holy Spirit, so James was tasked to bring correction to their error. He addressed them by saying:

> Ye adulterers and adulteresses, know ye not that the friendship of the world is enmity with God? whosoever therefore will be a friend of the world is the enemy of God.
>
> — James 4:4

When you read this verse in the original Greek text, it doesn't say, "Ye adulterers and adulteresses." It simply says, "You adulteresses," and this difference is important because James was speaking to the Church. In Greek, the "Church" is always grammatically in the feminine case and referred to as the Bride of Christ. The fact that James was calling the Church — who is betrothed to Christ and is His Bride — adulteresses means the believers were doing something very perverse.

Keep in mind, he was writing to Jews who had become Christians. Among the Jews, adultery was worthy of death. In fact, those committing adultery could be stoned to death. When James called these Jewish believers adulteresses, it was extremely offensive and must have felt like a slap up the side of their heads. Still, they were doing something that he said was the equivalent of spiritual adultery.

After James called these believers adulteresses, he went on to say, "…Know ye not that the friendship of the world is enmity with God?" (James 4:4). The Greek text here actually means, "Don't you know? Have you not comprehended? Do you not understand by now that the friendship of the world is enmity with God?"

'Friendship With the World' Is Spiritual Adultery

The word "friendship" in James 4:4 is important. In Greek, it is the word *philia*, and it denotes *friendship*. More specifically, it describes *a reciprocal relationship or affection*. Its use here indicates that these believers had entered into a reciprocal relationship with the world.

In Greek, the word "world" is a form of *kosmos*, which describes *every system or institution of the world*, such as *fashion, entertainment, education, politics, and more*. It indicates *every part of the world*. Although these believers that James was writing to started out white-hot in their passion for Jesus, something had caused them to begin drifting away from their devotion to Him.

In place of their love for the Lord, they began entering into a partnership or friendship with the world and all the world's systems. These actions so grieved the mind and heart of God that James addressed them by saying, "You adulteresses! You've given a part of yourself to the world that belongs only to the Holy Spirit!"

When you cross that line, in the mind of God, you have committed spiritual adultery.

None of us want to commit spiritual adultery against God or the Holy Spirit, but when we give our affection, attention, and devotion to the world and its systems and the things it provides more than to the Holy Spirit, we have crossed a line that we are not supposed to cross.

Loving the World More Than God Puts Us in Opposition With Him

Looking again at James 4:4, James wrote, "…Know ye not that the friendship of the world is enmity with God?" In other words, "A reciprocal relationship with the world is enmity with God." In this verse, the word "enmity" is the horrible Greek word *ecthra*, which describes *hostility* or *opposition between two people*. This is the word used in the gospels to describe the *hostile relationship* between Herod the Great and Pilate. History tells us that prior to their interaction over how to handle Jesus, they were arch enemies.

Thus the use of this word *ecthra* in the context of James 4:4 tells us when we as believers are mingling with the world — giving the world and all it offers more attention, devotion, and passion than we are giving with the Lord — we've entered into a reciprocal relationship with the world, and two dreadful conditions result:

First, James said this makes us *adulteresses*. We've crossed a line we weren't supposed to cross.

Second, James said it puts us *in hostility or opposition with God.*

Basically, James said, "Do you not understand? Have you not gotten it yet? When you give your passion, your attention, and your affection to the world and everything in it, entering into a reciprocal relationship with it, you put yourself in hostility and opposition with God."

Be Careful Not To Talk Yourself Out of Relationship With Jesus

James goes on to say, "…Whosoever therefore will be a friend of the world is the enemy of God" (James 4:4). Notice the phrase "will be." It is a translation of the unique Greek word *boulomai*, which means *I advise* or *I counsel*. This word pictures *the process of coaxing oneself or counseling oneself into something.* James' use of this word here describes *a believer who was once white-hot with love for Jesus but over time has gradually talked himself out of relationship with Jesus and back into relationship with the world.*

The people James was talking about — the ones committing spiritual adultery — began to advise themselves, coax themselves, or counsel themselves into believing that flirting with the world just a little bit might not be so bad. When we insert the meaning of the word *boulomai* — translated here as "will be" — into James 4:4, we could translate it to say:

Whosoever therefore coaxes himself, counsels himself, and talks himself into believing that it's okay to be a friend with the world is an enemy of God.

This tells us that people don't just wake up and suddenly backslide in one day. Becoming an enemy of God is a process. Little by little, a person coaches, counsels, and coaxes themselves into a compromised position. They talk to themselves saying things like, *I know that the Lord has told me not to watch those movies that have this and that in it, but everyone else is watching them. Maybe it's not so bad.*

Over a process of time, they talk and gradually walk themselves out of a white-hot relationship with Jesus and into a backslidden position where they're loving and relating to the world the way that they used to before they came to Christ. Through James, God says that when we do this, we've crossed a line we're not supposed to cross, and we've committed spiritual adultery.

Those who act in such a way make themselves "…the enemy of God" (James 4:4). This is the second time in this verse that James made this sobering statement. Whoever talks himself into being a friend of the world — entering a reciprocal relationship of affection and attention with the world and everything it offers — that person makes himself the enemy of God.

Friend, this means when you gradually and progressively walk away from the Lord and you begin to give your devotion, your passion, and your affection to other things more than to Him, you put yourself on the wrong side of the line and establish yourself to be in a hostile and adversarial position with God.

Make Jesus Your Main Focus, Not the World or Its Things

You may be thinking, *Well, how am I not supposed to connect with the world? I have to go to work, and I need to buy food and clothing and take care of my family. What does all this mean?* Of course you need to do these things, and God wants you to provide for your family. When the Bible warns against being "a friend of the world," it's talking about having a reciprocal relationship in which the world's systems and its material goods become your chief focus, rather than serving Jesus and Him being your chief focus.

Think about it. When your excitement and anticipation for the newest movies and music supersedes your excitement for the Lord, something's wrong. When you're more interested in the latest fashions and getting the newest phone upgrade than you are exploring God's Word, praying in the Spirit, and seeing Him move, you have become a friend of the world and are in hostile opposition to God.

Again, this transition is not sudden. It is a slow drift, a step-by-step movement in which a believer begins to coax himself and counsel himself into believing that flirting and playing with the world just a little may not be so bad. But James said that if you talk yourself into a relationship with the world, you put yourself in a hostile and adversarial position with God.

When we factor in the original Greek meaning of the key words in this verse, the *Renner Interpretive Version* (*RIV*) of James 4:4 is:

> **You adulteresses, don't you understand very clearly that a reciprocal relationship and friendship with the world — being enmeshed in its affairs — puts you in an adversarial and hostile position with God? If, then, anyone, and I really mean *anyone*, has talked himself into believing it's all right to be a companion in a reciprocal relationship with the world — that person, by his wrong choices, has made himself to be an enemy of God. His choices and actions have put him in a position that is completely contrary to and hostile toward God.**

The Holy Spirit Takes Up Permanent Residency in Us

James continued his teaching on the effects of being a friend of this world and an enemy of God, telling us:

> **Do ye think that the scripture saith in vain, The spirit that dwelleth in us lusteth to envy?**
> — James 4:5

In the original Greek text, this verse says, "Do you think that the Scripture says *to no purpose* that THE Spirit that dwells in us lusts to envy?" The fact that the definite article "the" is included here indicates James is talking about THE Holy Spirit of God.

There are three additional words that are very important in this verse. The first is the word "dwell," which is the Greek word *katoikeo*, a compound of the words *kata* and *oikeo*. The word *kata* means *down*, and *oikeo* is from the Greek word *oikos*, meaning *house*, but in the form *oikeo*, it means *to live*. When joined together to form *katoikeo*, it describes *a person settled down in a new home making it his permanent residency*.

This individual is so comfortable and at home, he's rolled out his own carpets, hung his own pictures, brought in his easy chair, and has nestled down in it. It is as if he says, "I am so at home here that I'm just going to settle down and make this my permanent residency." According to James 4:5, that is what the Holy Spirit does the moment we get saved. When we are born again, the Spirit of God enters our spirit and becomes a permanent indweller in you and me, which means our hearts are not hotels, and He is not a guest.

When He came in, He recreated our spirit and fashioned us into a temple so magnificent that He was pleased to dwell in it. He settled down, took up residency, became a permanent indweller in us. His desire is to exude all His power, all His glory, and all His fruit in and through our lives.

The Holy Spirit
Yearns for Our Devotion

When a believer violates the presence of the Holy Spirit in his life by flirting with the world or enmeshing himself in the things of the world, the Bible says, "...The spirit that dwelleth in us lusteth to envy" (James 4:5).

The word "lusteth" here is the strong Greek word *epipotheo*, which depicts *someone longing for something with such intensity that he is doubled over, hankering for it, longing for it, and pining for it.* Normally, this word is used to indicate an intense yearning for something that is morally wrong and sinful. But in James 4:5, the word *epipotheo* describes the intense yearning that the Holy Spirit has to have us entirely for Himself.

To be clear, this doesn't mean you can't have a good job, take good care of your spouse and children, or experience the joys of having a nice home or going on a vacation. It just means when it comes to your devotion, the Holy Spirit wants to be *number one*. He has settled down and taken up permanent residency in you, and He wants to be top priority. If you share your highest devotion with something or someone other than Him, it will send Him into a state where He's ready to do whatever is necessary to break that attraction and bring you back to Himself.

The Holy Spirit Will Fight
To Be First in Our Life

Along with the Holy Spirit being doubled over, yearning and pining for us, James went on to say that the Spirit experiences "envy" regarding us. This word "envy" is the Greek word *phthonos*, which depicts *intense jealousy, such as what a man feels when he discovers his wife has committed adultery.* Rather than just say goodbye and end the relationship, this man is going to do everything he can to get his wife back.

Thus the word *phthonos* — translated as "envy" in James 4:5 — pictures a rescue operation or plan in which the Holy Spirit is willing to do whatever it takes to break our love affair with other things and bring us back home to Himself. It doesn't matter how much we surrender to Him today, tomorrow He's going to ask for more. He's yearning for us and wants every single part of us. That's why James said in verse four, "Don't you understand? Have you not yet comprehended that the Spirit of God lives inside you? And the Spirit in you is doubled over, yearning, and pining to have your greatest devotion."

When we factor in the original Greek meaning of the key words in this verse, the *Renner Interpretive Version* (*RIV*) of James 4:5 is:

Do you suppose the Scripture says to no purpose that the Spirit has settled down, taken up residency, permanently dwells inside us, and is filled with an intense jealousy anytime we give our devotion to someone or something else? In fact, the Holy Spirit so passionately pines and yearns for us [that He is not willing for us to share our highest devotion with anyone or anything else more than with Him].

Friend, the Holy Spirit loves you intensely and has done such a marvelous work in you, the last thing you would want to do is disregard His affection, embrace the world, and hear Him call you an adulterer or an adulteress. Therefore you need to embrace the Spirit of God in your life — welcome Him, accommodate Him, and live a life that is worthy of His indwelling presence. That is what we read about in James 4:4-5.

If you want to honor the presence of the Spirit of God in your life, take time to pray:

Holy Spirit, help me to understand who You really are. I welcome Your presence and want to honor You in every area of my life. Forgive me when I've crossed the line and become more in love with the things of this world than with You. I ask You to fully release Your power, Your glory, Your character, and Your fruit in my life. I want to accommodate You and make You feel at home in me. In Jesus' name. Amen.

STUDY QUESTIONS

Study to shew thyself approved unto God, a workman that
needeth not to be ashamed, rightly dividing the word of truth.
— 2 Timothy 2:15

1. We learned in James 4:5 that the Holy Spirit takes up permanent residency in us the moment we are born again. To really solidify this truth in your heart, consider these amazing verses and note how they reinforce and elaborate on this fabulous fact.

    • John 14:16-17,23

    • Romans 8:11

    • Galatians 4:6

    • 1 John 3:24; 4:13

    • 1 Corinthians 3:16; 1 Corinthians 6:19; 2 Corinthians 6:16

2. The believers James wrote to had started out white-hot in their passion for Jesus, but something caused them to drift away from their devotion to Him. Who did Jesus talk to in Revelation 2:1-7 about "leaving their first love?" What is the only remedy Jesus offered them — and *you* — to make things right again? (Also *consider* Isaiah 55:6-7; Joel 2:12-13; Acts 3:19; 1 John 1:9.)

PRACTICAL APPLICATION

But be ye doers of the word, and not hearers only,
deceiving your own selves.
— James 1:22

1. According to James 4:4, when a person backslides from his or her love and devotion to Christ, it is a gradual process. Little by little, a person coaches, counsels, and coaxes himself into a compromised position. Does this describe *you?* Are there things in this world that you're more attracted to than Jesus? Have you grown more in love with this world's entertainment and its pleasures than the Lord? Take time to allow the Holy Spirit to truly search your heart and show you what's going on inside (*see* Psalm 139:23-24).

2. What is the Holy Spirit putting His finger on in your life? What have you allowed — even unknowingly — to usurp the number-one position that belongs only to Him?

3. Take time now to repent and pray the prayer at the end of this lesson. Welcome the Holy Spirit back into first place in your life and ask Him to show you what you need to do to continually experience His deep love for you.

A Prayer To Receive Salvation

If you've never received Jesus as your Savior and Lord, now is the time for you to experience the new life Jesus wants to give you! To receive God's gift of salvation that can be obtained through Jesus alone, pray this prayer from your heart:

Jesus, I repent of my sin and receive You as my Savior and Lord. Wash away my sin with Your precious blood and make me completely new. I thank You that my sin is removed, and Satan no longer has any right to lay claim on me. Through Your empowering grace, I faithfully promise that I will serve You as my Lord for the rest of my life.

If you just prayed this prayer of salvation, you are born again! You are a brand-new creation in Christ! Would you please let us know of your decision by going to **renner.org/salvation**? We would love to connect with you and pray for you as you begin your new life in Christ.

Scriptures for further study: John 3:16; John 14:6; Acts 4:12; Ephesians 1:7; Hebrews 10:19,20; 1 Peter 1:18,19; Romans 10:9,10; Colossians 1:13; 2 Corinthians 5:17; Romans 6:4; 1 Peter 1:3

Notes

_____

_____

_____

_____

_____

_____

_____

_____

_____

_____

_____

_____

_____

_____

_____

_____

_____

_____

_____

_____

_____

_____

_____

_____

_____

_____

_____

_____

CLAIM YOUR FREE RESOURCE!

As a way of introducing you further to the teaching ministry of Rick Renner, we would like to send you FREE of charge his teaching, "How To Receive a Miraculous Touch From God" on CD or as an MP3 download.

In His earthly ministry, Jesus commonly healed *all* who were sick of *all* their diseases. In this profound message, learn about the manifold dimensions of Christ's wisdom, goodness, power, and love toward all humanity who came to Him in faith with their needs.

☑ **YES, I want to receive Rick Renner's monthly teaching letter!**

Simply scan the QR code to claim this resource or go to: **renner.org/claim-your-free-offer**

Connect WITH US!